MIDLAND SCOTTISH BUSES

Walter Burt

AMBERLEY PUBLISHING

First published 2014

Amberley Publishing
The Hill, Stroud
Gloucestershire, GL5 4EP

www.amberley-books.com

Copyright © Walter Burt, 2014

The right of Walter Burt to be identified as the
Author of this work has been asserted in accordance
with the Copyrights, Designs and Patents Act 1988.

ISBN 978 1 4456 3466 1 (PRINT)
ISBN 978 1 4456 3476 0 (EBOOK)

British Library Cataloguing in Publication Data.
A catalogue record for this book is available from
the British Library.

Typeset in 9.5pt on 12pt Celeste.
Typesetting by Amberley Publishing.
Printed in the UK.

Introduction

In this book, I will take a walk down memory lane and take a look at some of the vehicles to have worked in the old Midland Scottish operating area, the home of the former Walter Alexander bus empire. You will find that the bulk of the images are from the 'glory days' of the Scottish Bus Group, an era in our own lifetime when people remember when the buses were azure blue and cream. I will start by looking at a few of the buses that operated with Alexander's, including Lawson's of Kirkintilloch, up until Walter Alexander's bus company split into the three separate operating companies of Midland, Fife and Northern on 15 May 1961.

Here is a brief summary of what happened since then. In September 1963, Scottish Omnibuses Group (Holdings) Ltd, which was renamed from Walter Alexander after the 1961 split, was itself renamed to become Scottish Bus Group Ltd. The group consisted of seven bus companies. They were: Scottish Omnibuses Ltd, Central SMT Co. Ltd, Western SMT Co. Ltd, Highland Omnibuses Ltd, W. Alexander & Sons (Midland) Ltd, W. Alexander & Sons (Northern) Ltd and W. Alexander & Sons (Fife) Ltd. These seven companies remained as the Scottish Bus Group until 1985, when the group decided to restructure. When the bus group did restructure, four more companies were created, along with the fledgling Citylink company. They were Clydeside, Kelvin, Strathtay, and Lowland Scottish.

We will start by having a look at some of the vehicles that were operating within the Midland operating area in the years leading up to the 1961 split. We will continue to look at some of the various other buses, coaches and ancillary vehicles to have served within the Midland operating area as they were introduced. It is my hope that this book will not only appeal to the local bus enthusiast, but perhaps also to those interested in seeing how central Scotland looked between the 1960s and the mid-1990s. I have also included a look at a few of the vehicle types to have worked since then with the area's current bus operator, FirstBus. Most of the images I have chosen are in colour, but there are a few good black and white images included too, mainly because of the subject matter or, to a lesser extent, because there may be something interesting within the photograph itself. Whenever possible, I have included the bus registration and fleet numbers of the vehicles in the photographs, as vehicles may appear more than once in the book with a different registration or fleet number. The main aim of this book is to show a combination of chassis and body types, as well as looking at the various livery and fleet name variations and changes that have been seen over the years. It is by no means a comprehensive history of the company or its vehicles, as many vehicles types are not included in these pages. It is hoped that what I have done is to stir some memories for readers, both young and old alike.

Brief Description

Walter Alexander's company was formally registered as a bus operator on 23 May 1924, but he had actually been operating buses since 1913 from his cycle shop premises in Camelon, Falkirk. Walter Alexander had also started from about this date to build bus bodies, mainly for his own growing fleet, but gradually for other operators too. The bus building operations became a separate company in 1947, after the Labour government's Transport Act of that year, and from then on it is another story. Alexander's was only one of a handful of operators vying for trade in an age of great competition since chassis were made available after the Great War. Most of the smaller operators didn't last long, though, many being absorbed by the larger operators until they too were absorbed. Gradually, the main operator in the Central Belt became the Falkirk-based Walter Alexander & Sons Ltd. Their operations would eventually stretch from Glasgow and Oban in the south and west to the north-east of Scotland. Their operating areas were known as the Southern, Fife and Northern areas. The Southern area subsequently became the Midland operating area after the 1961 split.

At this time, all Alexander's buses wore an attractive azure blue livery with one, two, or sometimes three cream relief bands between decks. Their coach livery was 'the opposite' as they were cream liveried, usually with an azure blue roof and relief bands.

Alexander's buses carried their fleet numbers and garage shed codes on small square plates, usually on the front and rear of each vehicle, but sometimes on the front nearside too, on the older half-cab type of vehicles. The depots which have housed Midlands buses over the years were, or are, at Alloa (A), Balfron (B), Bannockburn (BN), Crieff (C), Callander (CL), Cumbernauld (CD), Grangemouth (G), Kilsyth (K), Kirkintilloch (KH), Larbert (L), Linlithgow (LW), Milngavie (M), Oban (ON), Perth (P), Pitlochry (PY), Stepps (SS) and Stirling (S). The head office for the Midland Scottish operating area was located in Brown Street, Camelon, Falkirk. Callander depot served as an outstation of Stirling from 1967. Oban depot was transferred to Highland Omnibuses in 1970, but would find its way back into Midland's hands about ten years later. The depot at Stirling closed in 1983, with Bannockburn taking over its remaining duties. Because the Scottish Bus Group was restructuring in 1985, in readiness for deregulation the following year, many changes would take place within Midland Scottish buses. Linlithgow depot was obtained from Eastern Scottish while Crieff, Perth and Pitlochry depots were passed over to the new Strathtay Scottish group in Tayside. Midland lost about 300 buses when the depots in Cumbernauld, Kilsyth, Kirkintilloch, Milngavie and Stepps were passed over to help form the new Kelvin Scottish Omnibuses.

When Walter Alexander's split into the three operating companies in 1961, Midland's buses remained in the azure blue and cream livery, with the only change being to the fleet name, with the addition of the word 'Midland'. When the three new companies chose their liveries in 1962, W. Alexander (Midland), as the company had now become, kept the traditional azure blue and cream livery, with the fleet name simply being abbreviated to the word 'Midland' in a script style of lettering. The 'Bluebird' fleet name for coach services was retained, along with the famous bluebird emblem. The split also spelt the end for the red liveries of David Lawson, as the company was absorbed into the main Midland fleet, and of the buses serving Perth City Centre, as over the next few years they were all repainted into Midland's blue and cream colours.

The fleet name has changed many times over the years since 1961. Over the next year or so, the buses would be found with the 'Midland' fleet name applied in a script style of lettering, but by 1965 this was changed again to a Walter Alexander-inspired large block style of fleet name, but saying 'Midland' instead of 'Alexander'. This was changed again in 1968 when the fleet name style changed to a rather neat looking lower case type, but still saying 'Midland'. This style of fleet name remained in use for ten years as in 1978 Midland adopted the corporate style of name and would now be known as Midland Scottish. The corporate fleet name included a three-quarters saltire in between the words 'Midland' and 'Scottish', and was the style of fleet name adopted by all the Scottish Bus Group companies at the time. There would be further changes around 1990 as the company was experimenting with fleet name styles for 'Bluebird' and 'Midland Bluebird'. Although the Midland Bluebird name had previously been applied to some of the company's coaches, this would be like a re-vamped style to be used as the company fleet name. The Midland Bluebird name was retained for a while by the new owners of the company when it was sold to GRT Group in September 1990. The former operations of Midland Scottish are today part of First Edinburgh, trading simply as First, after being merged with neighbouring First subsidiaries SMT (Eastern Scottish) and Lowland Buses. The Bluebird emblem has unfortunately all but disappeared from the buses serving the former area of Alexander (Midland).

As you will probably have noticed from the locations of the bus depots, the Midland operating area covered a large swathe of central Scotland. It operated a network of services, not just from its home in Falkirk but also the neighbouring places such as Stirling, Alloa, Grangemouth, and of course Glasgow. By the very nature of the vast areas covered, the Midland company provided bus services to a large amount of rural locations in Perthshire and Stirlingshire, as well as to the new, large sprawling housing estates springing up around Glasgow such as Drumchapel. The company also operated an extensive tour programme, offering both day trips and extensive tour packages. Midland also operated longer distance routes, many to the Western Isles, but also to places such as St Andrews in Fife, a popular holiday destination for many Glaswegians in the 1950s and 1960s. In fact, all of Midland's services to and from Fife were run in co-operation with its sister company, Alexander (Fife). Services also ran even further, to places such as Oban, Inverness and Aberdeen.

Because of the various extremities of the company's routes, Midland operated a great variety of vehicle types. Leyland and Guy were the principal double deck bus types operated by Walter Alexander before the 1961 split. Other double deck types were introduced into the fleet, such as the Albion Lowlander and the Bristol Lodekka and, eventually, the Daimler Fleetline although the Lowlander never turned out to be anything special of note. The double deck buses were usually found on the more densely populated routes, especially around Glasgow and the busy town networks around Falkirk and Stirling. Most of the single deck buses were Leyland vehicles, but there were also a handful of other vehicles too, such as the Alexander-bodied Bristol LH, AEC Reliance and Albion Viking. There were also a good number of Fords and a few Bedfords. The various body types should all be seen in the pages of this book. Eventually, the Leyland Leopard would be the standard single decker, with the Daimler Fleetline being the predominant double deck bus. Minibuses started to infiltrate into the Midland fleet in the mid-

1980s, in readiness for the impending deregulation and privatisation of the bus industry, and were successful in areas such as the local services around Oban, Alloa and Falkirk.

Since 1990, when Midland Scottish was privatised, GRT/FirstBus have more or less made the Scania their chassis of choice, although they have bought other types in smaller batches, namely Mercedes-Benz, Dennis Dart and the Volvo B7 and B10 types. The body of choice is now that produced by Wrightbus, who are based in Ballymena, Northern Ireland. Other vehicles have been seen; fleet movements within the group can throw up the odd surprise or two every now and again. It is such a shame that nowadays the former Midland Scottish bus company buy their vehicles of choice from Scania with Wright bodies when they have on their doorstep, in Glasgow Road, Falkirk, one of the leading bus builders in the industry, whose roots are firmly entrenched in the story of Midland Scottish buses.

Acknowledgements

Once again, I thank the following people for their contributions to this book. I have chosen images from trusted sources who between them have gathered a fantastic record of the vehicles to have served the former Alexander (Midland) operating area. The bulk of the photographs belong to my good friend Robert Dickson, but the other contributors receive just as much by way of heartfelt thanks. In no particular order, my thanks go to Robert Dickson, Paul Redmond, Paris-Roubaix, Len Wright, Michelle O'Connell, Stephen Dowle, Dr George Fairbairn, Berisford Jones, Clive A. Brown, Malcolm Audsley, Malcolm Jones and David McGeachan.

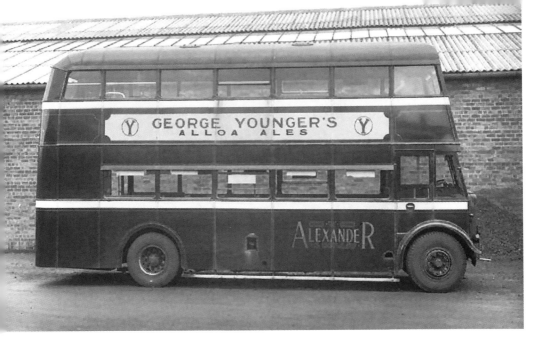

A grand off-side view is afforded to us of a Guy Arab 2 with Northern Counties utility bodywork dating from 1944/5. Seven of these vehicles were purchased in 1944, with only one bought the following year. All these vehicles had the same H30/26R layout and operated on Perth City Transport services with a specific red livery. All eight vehicles were withdrawn in 1963. (Author's Collection)

One of the all-Leyland PD2/12s that were purchased by Alexander's in 1951 is seen here parked up in Glasgow. DMS 351 (RB 117) was eventually withdrawn in 1970, but saw a further four years working as a driver training vehicle with Aberdeen Corporation as their fleet number 97. It was sold on once more in 1974 to Alexander (Greyhound) of Arbroath. (Author's Collection)

Seen here parked up in Alloa early in 1962, we find BMS 105 (A71), a 1947 AEC Regal with Burlingham B35F bodywork. It appears to be a Grangemouth allocated vehicle so it must be laying over between runs. It was withdrawn and sold on to a Glasgow-based dealer in 1965. AEC traditionally had the model type on the radiator, and this can be seen by the word 'Regal' in script type lettering. (Paul Redmond)

A rare view inside the workshop area at Alloa depot finds Burlingham-bodied Daimler CVD6, BMS 416 (D21). This is also early in 1962 as the vehicle has yet to receive its 'M' fleet number prefix letter, but is now in the hands of Alexander (Midland). This vehicle was withdrawn and sold to Highland Omnibuses, where it only spent another two years in service. (Paul Redmond)

Another Daimler CVD6 is seen here at an undisclosed location between the summers of 1961 and 1962. DMS 557 (D44) wore a very distinctive Eastern Coach Works 'Queen Mary' body style from 1951. It was allocated to Grangemouth depot until its withdrawal in 1965. It saw a further two years' service with a local Penrith operator, E. Hartness. (Paul Redmond)

AMS 534 (MG4) was an attractive looking Guy Arab 3 with Duple body work. New in 1947, it ran in the Lawson fleet from 1949 until May 1961, when it was absorbed into the new Alexander (Midland) fleet. This Kilsyth-based vehicle is seen in Glasgow's Dundas Street bus station between runs to Lenzie. MG4 was withdrawn in 1965 and sold for further use to a local contractor. (Paul Redmond)

Alexander-bodied Leyland LT5A WG 2392 (P723) is shown here in this 1959 photograph while working with Lawson's. It was new in 1935 with the fleet number N205 but was re-numbered to P723 when it had a larger replacement engine fitted in 1945. Five months after being re-engined, it was then re-bodied by Alexander, but to the same B36F layout. It was sold to Lawson's in 1953, but did not make it back into the Alexander fleet in 1961, when the Alexander empire was split into the three operating areas. (Paris-Roubaix)

A couple of golden oldies parked up in Larbert depot, c. 1962. On the left is WG 9325 (P635), a 1940 Leyland TS8 with Alexander B39F body work. This vehicle was withdrawn in 1964, making it one of the oldest vehicles in the fleet, having served for Alexander's for twenty-four years. The vehicle on the right, CMS 208 (PA139), is a 1949 Leyland PS1 with Alexander C35F body work. This was withdrawn in 1967 but ended up in Dundee with the 'Children's Free Breakfast and City Mission'. (Paul Redmond)

Falkirk bus station is the location for this photograph as we find BWG 316 (PA90), a 1948 Leyland PS1, again with an Alexander C35F body. A few shoppers are seen boarding for the homeward journey to Grangemouth after a day in the town centre as a conductress makes her way to her vehicle, perhaps the Albion Lowlander seen ahead of PA90. PA90 was withdrawn in 1968, having served with Alexander's for twenty hard-working years. (Paul Redmond)

Another long-serving member of the Alexander fleet was WG 9544 (R315). It was an all-Leyland TD7, which was new in 1941. It is seen here among a myriad of various other vehicle types in Falkirk depot, although it is seen to be wearing a Grangemouth depot plate. Withdrawn in 1964, it was sold to the Bellshill & Mossend Scrap Metal Company for scrap. (Paul Redmond)

Another visit to Falkirk bus station at Callendar Riggs, around late 1961, and we find AMS 110 (RO469), a 1944 Daimler CWA6 with Brush L27/26R body work. It is seen with the traditional panel lining but has no cream relief bands, only cream panelling where the adverts are applied. It is also seen with the fleet name, which was altered to include the word 'Midland' in brackets before the Midland script style of fleet name was adopted the following year. (Paul Redmond)

Leyland PD1, MRA5, started life in 1948 registered as BMS 316 and with a Burlingham L27/26R body. This body was transferred from an ex-Ribble Leyland TD4. In 1955, it received its new Alexander body and was re-registered HMS 219, as seen here in Glasgow, displaying one of the typical adverts of the time for milk. It was stationed at Milngavie depot by the time it was withdrawn in 1967. (Len Wright)

Leyland PD1 Titan AWG 367 (MRA29) is seen parked up in Glasgow, having arrived on a service from Gartcosh. This Stepps-based vehicle was new to Alexander's in 1948 and carried the company's own L27/26R bodywork. This vehicle saw twenty years service with the company, being withdrawn in 1968. (Len Wright)

Glasgow's Dundas Street bus station, which closed in 1976, is the scene for AWG 549 (MPA14), an Alexander-bodied Leyland Tiger PS1 of 1947 vintage. It looks about ready to depart on a service 174 to Hillhead, a housing estate in Kirkintilloch, which was a half-hourly service often operated by Lodekkas. This bus was withdrawn in 1968, only a few years after being photographed, and still looks in great condition for its age. (Len Wright)

An Alexander-bodied Leyland Titan PD2/3 of 1951 vintage takes a well-earned break in the yard at its home depot of Stepps during August 1966. It was withdrawn four years later in 1970, making it one of the oldest buses in the Midland fleet at the time. I am unsure as to which vehicle the chassis on the right hand side of the Titan belonged. I know that Midland had a liking for stripping their withdrawn vehicles to the bone to obtain spare parts. This vehicle carries the large block style of fleet name, mentioned in the introduction pages, similar to that used by Alexander. (Robert Dickson Collection)

On the left of this image is Alexander-bodied Leyland PD1 BWG 78 (MRA33), which was new in 1948 and served in the southern (Midland) area for twenty years, working from Milngavie depot. It is accompanied by KWG 648 (MRB187), an Alexander-bodied Leyland PD3 from 1958, also stationed at Milngavie. This vehicle looks better with the application of three cream relief bands. (Len Wright)

Numerically the last of the 1958 PD3s, KWG 664 (MRB203) makes its way along Fettercairn Avenue, Drumchapel, in 1970. I would suggest that this and the vehicle following close behind are on school runs as the street looks busy with kids in school uniform. Nothing in this photograph remains as MRB203 was withdrawn in the mid-1970s and Fettercairn Avenue has itself been redeveloped in recent years. (Michelle O'Connell)

Glasgow Dundas Street bus station, once home to Lawson's bus services, is the location for this photograph of RMS 687 (MRB255). This 1961 PD3/3C Leyland Titan had a chassis constructed from parts taken from older Leyland PS1 Tigers and an engine from Leyland OPS2/1 Tigers. This vehicle was withdrawn in 1976. (Len Wright)

This curvaceous looking vehicle was a 1953 Bedford SB with Burlingham C24F bodywork. EMS 835 (MW252) is pictured beside its stable mate inside Perth depot and was used more-or-less on tour work. This vehicle was sold on in 1966, seeing service with a further two operators until being finally withdrawn in 1970. The interiors would have been well illuminated due to the curved roof windows along the sides of the vehicle too. (Paul Redmond)

JWG 86 (MRD31), a Bristol LD6G from 1957, is seen here parked up inside Kilsyth depot. This bus operated in the fleet of David Lawson but was absorbed into the Midland fleet when Lawson's were taken over in May 1961. It was still being used on a route (service 170) which was traditionally one of Lawson's. It remained in the Midland fleet until withdrawal in 1972. This vehicle is also seen to be carrying the large block style fleet name, as previously mentioned. (Robert Dickson Collection)

Another Bristol LD6G is pictured while in the service of Lawson's. GWG 995 (RD19) was one of the 1956 intake of vehicles and is having a rest in Glasgow, having completed a run on the circular service 172 to Kirkintilloch via Bishopbriggs and Auchinairn. Like the previous vehicle, this too ended up being absorbed into the Midland fleet, where it served until withdrawal in 1971. (Robert Dickson Collection)

Our third offering of an LD6G Lodekka also shows a former Lawson's vehicle. KWG 601 (MRD72) operated in the Lawson's fleet from 1959 until 1961, when it was also absorbed into the Midland fleet. When photographed here, it was working from Perth depot, where it had apparently recently been on a local service 31C between Mill Street and Letham Upper. (Author's Collection)

This bus is TWG 531 (MRD161), a Bristol FLF-type Lodekka of the Alexander Midland subsidiary of the Scottish Bus Group. It is seen swinging out into the traffic from Dunfermline's upper bus station on Saturday 7 May 1977. The bus is heading for Edinburgh on the 55 service. It is probably covering a breakdown in Perth of a Dunfermline bus on the 55, which at that time ran from Perth through Kinross, Kelty and Dunfermline to Edinburgh. (Stephen Dowle)

Something you never see nowadays is a bus, in particular a double decker, with streamers hanging from every window. These vehicles looked better with the black lining applied at the edges of the cream relief bands. RVW 393D (MRD197) and AMS 9B (MRD191) are seen parked up in Alva, a popular summer picnic place at the bottom of the Ochil Hills in Clackmannanshire. One of the drivers can just be seen at the rear of the vehicle, taking advantage of the glorious summer weather during a hot 1977. (Bob Dickson)

A beautiful midsummer evening in June 1979 finds us at Glasgow Buchanan bus station. Bristol FLF Lodekka UEV 220E (MRD208) is seen here. This bus had come to Scotland from Eastern National in 1971 as part of the SBG's exchange of Bristol VRTs for National Bus Company FLFs. Since its arrival, it acquired a destination aperture of SBG pattern. Sliding window vents alternate with the 'hopper' windows in both upper and lower saloons. (Stephen Dowle)

Another of the buses involved in the Anglo-Scottish VRT/FLF exchanges that had come from the fleet of Eastern National in 1971 was RWC 942D (MRD200). Allocated to Kirkintilloch depot, it is seen not long after arrival from Eastern National as it is still using the standard Tilling Group destination display. It will also be noted that they had the Cave-Browne-Cave heating intake louvers, a feature not used on the new Scottish vehicles. (Author's Collection)

Once again, RWC 942D (MRD200) is the subject matter as we find it now with the traditional SBG destination display. It appears to be a rather sparsely populated service as we see it in Kyle Street, Glasgow, shortly after leaving Buchanan bus station on 18 May 1978. It is heading for Lenzie, possibly on a local service 171. (Stephen Dowle)

VWG 360 (MRD180) is sitting in stance 4 at Dundas Street bus station in Glasgow, having loaded a few customers for the journey to Auchinairn. The service 177 was a fairly frequent service and only took about twenty minutes. MRD180 was withdrawn at the end of 1978 and sold for scrap. (Author's Collection)

Dundas Street bus station is seen here again, with LD6G Lodekka GWG 993 (MRD17), a Kirkintilloch-based vehicle, ready to depart on one of the former Lawson routes to Campsie Glen via Kirkintilloch. This bus was new in 1956 and was part of the Lawson fleet until May 1961, when Lawson's was absorbed into the new Alexander (Midland) company. All Lawson's services used Dundas Street and Alexander's continued those routes until Dundas Street closed about 1976. (Len Wright)

Still staying in Dundas Street bus station, Alexander-bodied Leyland Royal Tiger CMS 379 (MPC13) sits in an area adjacent to stance five shortly before leaving on a run along the West Coast to Oban. This Shotts allocated vehicle will make the journey to Oban in about four hours, including a refreshment stop en route. Due to this vehicle having a central door, room was available for two lucky travellers to get the best views of the trip, and it looks like a couple have already settled in their place at the front. (Len Wright)

Leyland Royal Tiger EMS 521 (MPC66) sits inside Perth depot in a rather clean condition, ready to be used on a tour or other private hire. This is due to the fact that the antimacassars are in place on the headrests, as was the practice at the time (Antimacassars were used to stop hair creams and other such products from spoiling the headrest area). The Alexander 'Coronation' body looks quite suited for the task and was bright inside. (Paul Redmond)

Another vehicle that was new in the Lawson fleet was this Alexander C29F bodied Albion MR9L, JMS 388 (N1). New in 1957, it served with Lawson's until they were absorbed into the new Alexander (Midland) company in 1961. It is seen here in Dundas Street bus station, still in its Lawson's livery, before heading off on a tour. Withdrawn in 1968, it had a further few years working for T. Weir of Whitburn. (Paul Redmond)

TWG 564 (MRE13) was an Alexander-bodied Albion Lowlander from the first batch, delivered in 1963. When you marry a Leyland PD3 front end to a low frame, the outcome is this beast. The front upper saloon seats sat too high and they can only just be seen in the photograph. It never proved to be a popular design combination. Alexander's Fife received a few with bodywork by Northern Counties, which seemed to suit the Lowlander better. (Stephen Dowle)

A much changed scene shows Albion Lowlander VWG 375 (MRE37) in Glasgow's Parliamentary Road on 15 May 1978. All of Midland's Lowlanders were bodied by Alexander's. This is one from the second batch, which had a different destination display layout and a much altered upper front saloon seating area. This was due to complaints about the front end layout of the first batch of Albions. (Stephen Dowle)

In June 1979, we find Albion Lowlander VWG 377 (MRE39) heading east out of Alloa along Clackmannan Road. In all probability, this is a workers' service from the nearby Paton's Mill, heading along the line of the route of the service 14. I have noticed that the workers' buses had route numbers and some displayed 'Private' while others displayed a location. (Robert Dickson)

Park Royal-bodied AEC Monocoach FMS 980 (MAC24) nears its destination of Glasgow's Killermont Street bus station with a heavy passenger load on a run from Balfron. The Alexander-bodied Leyland PD1 on the left, BWG 76 (MRA31), displays one of the adverts for Askit powders that were commonly found on buses during the 1950s and 1960s. The rear Alexander 'Garter' can just be made out on the lowest panel on the rear of MRA31. (Len Wright)

Back to Dundas Street bus station to see AEC Reliance RMS 738 (MAC204) sitting in stance 5, waiting to depart on a trip to Oban. This was a long journey, but it must have been quite relaxing sitting in this attractive-looking Alexander C41F coach. MAC204 was withdrawn in 1970, but was moved on to Highland Omnibuses, where no doubt it worked on similar routes. The large, distinctive Bluebird emblem on the wall was a well known feature in the bus stations used by Alexander's in Glasgow. (Len Wright)

Kilsyth depot allocated AEC Reliance VWG 351 (MAC213) was one of five delivered to Midland in 1963 which were the first ones to be built using the stylish Y Type body. It is seen here parked up at the layover area adjacent to the entrance to Dundas Street bus station in Glasgow. It is unusual for a tour bus in the 1960s not to have antimacassars fitted over the head rests like the coach on the left, which is also being used for a tour. (Author's Collection)

Taking centre stage while parked up in Glasgow is SWG 619 (MRB263). Not an Albion Lowlander as you might think at first glance, but an Alexander-bodied Leyland PD3. The 'St Helens' style of glass fibre front panel was quite confusing if you hadn't noticed the Leyland badge. These buses would depart from Buchanan Street on their respective services, the run to Stirling taking just over an hour and a quarter, while the run to Bo'ness, which would be in the charge of AMS 267B (MPE1), would take almost two hours to complete. (Len Wright)

A brief visit to the east coast brings us to Edinburgh's St Andrews Square bus station. On this particular occasion in 1975, Alexander Y Type-bodied Albion Viking JMS 455E (MNV41) was being used on shuttle duties between the bus station and the Royal Highland Show at Ingliston, to the west of the city centre. (Dr George Fairbairn)

This Alexander-bodied Viking is seen leaving Falkirk bus station in October 1980. LWG 898F (MNV55) was new to Alexander (Midland) in May 1968 and was based at Larbert depot, to the north-west of Falkirk, but wouldn't last too much longer as it was withdrawn not long after the photograph was taken. (Robert Dickson)

New in March 1967, Alloa-allocated Albion Viking HWG 526E (MNV23) is pictured with a healthy load in Main Street, Sauchie, in March 1981. It is believed that this was a workers' service from Paton's mill, just down the road in Alloa. At this point in time, MNV23 was the last Potter-bodied Viking in the Midland fleet. Midland's blue livery really suited the style of the Y Type body. (Robert Dickson)

A visit to Bannockburn depot in August 1879 finds Albion Viking JMS 453E (MNV38) sitting in between turns. This image shows the bus with the corporate style of Scottish Bus Group fleet name on the sides, but still carrying the older 'Midland' style fleet name on the front above the grill. You will also notice the rather sickly looking lime green colour of the moulded entrance steps. (Robert Dickson)

The driver on this particularly wintery day deserved full marks for making it to his starting point in Sauchie to begin a local school contract run in mid-January 1981. The bus was Alexander's bodied Albion Viking MWG 107F (MNV60), and as can be seen, I don't think many pupils would have bothered going to school that day. (Robert Dickson)

FWG 980D (MNV14) was one of the second batch of Albion Vikings, but one of the first batch that were completed by Potters in Belfast in 1966. It was wearing traditional coach livery when pictured at Grangemouth depot in September 1980. The vehicle is still wearing the second style of 'Midland' fleet name and would probably have never worn the corporate style of Midland Scottish logo as this was about the time that the Albion Vikings were being withdrawn from service. (Robert Dickson)

One of the Albion Viking buses allocated to Grangemouth depot is our subject, photographed in the depot yard during September 1980. JMS 459E (MNV44) was new in June 1967 but has now acquired a panel behind the front grille area. Nothing wrong with that at all; if anything, it doesn't look too bad, given that the panel seems to be from the side of one of the company's coaches and includes the Bluebird emblem too. (Robert Dickson)

This is HWG 522E (MNV19), one of the Albion Vikings allocated to Perth depot. This was one of the second batch of 1967 vehicles that were completed in Belfast by Potter. It is seen in the layover area at Perth bus station, having recently arrived either on a service 46 from Crieff or on one of the shorter runs from Dunning. It is also worth pointing out that it is one of only a few photographs I have seen of an Albion Viking with the small Saltire motif on the grille. (Author's Collection)

Our final look at the Alexander-bodied Viking affords us the opportunity to compare the rear end of the vehicles built by Alexander's themselves to the rear end as built by Potter's of Belfast. In this instance, HWG 526E (MNV23) on the left is the variant built by Potter's of Belfast, while JMS 457E (MNV42) on the right is the Alexander-bodied one. Both vehicles also show different layouts to the row of rear seats. (Robert Dickson)

Leyland Tiger Cub JMS 212 (PD94) is seen near the end of its run in Airdrie in 1961, working a service 78 from Falkirk via Allandale and Cumbernauld. I believe that it was just a few more yards up the road before the bus would have turned to the right and into the bus station. PD94 was bodied by Alexander with a B45F layout, although by the looks of it, forty-five seats were definitely not needed on this run. New to Alexander's in 1956, it was transferred into the Midland fleet in 1961 at the break up, where it stayed until withdrawal in 1972. (Paul Redmond)

RMS 701 (MPD212), a 1961 Alexander-bodied Leyland Tiger Cub is seen parked up on the dockside at a seaside resort, Dunoon perhaps, while on tour duty. This bus would have been flooded with light due to the side and front skylights as well as the two orange top lights. Due to the mould being destroyed in a fire at Alexander's, only nineteen of these buses were completed with this rather stylish bodywork. (Author's Collection)

I am one of those people who like to see the small differences between various vehicles of the same type. The Alexander bodywork on the Leyland tiger cub often showed small variations in the way the mouldings, badges or destination equipment were placed. TWG 580 (MPD226) is seen in Glasgow beside a stable mate, ready for tour duty, complete with antimacassars on the headrests. These coaches would have been ideal for tour work as they were bright and airy inside due to the skylight windows. (Author's Collection)

Alexander-bodied Leyland Tiger Cub TWG 597 (MPD243) is seen coming off the ferry at Kyle of Lochalsh, on the way back from the Isle of Skye. The date was August 1976 and on this particular day, the sun shone brightly during an otherwise driech summer that year. This ferry terminal is located just to the west of the town's railway station and MPD was still giving sterling service after fourteen years. (Berisford Jones)

Another photograph taken in Parliamentary Road, Glasgow, during May 1978 shows TWG 585 (MPD231), an Alexander-bodied PSUC1/2 Leyland Tiger Cub, on a local service from Buchanan bus station to Tallant Road, Drumchapel, via Anniesland. This rather grubby looking bus, new in 1962, was stationed at Milngavie depot and was near to being withdrawn. A solitary Ford Cortina is the only other vehicle to be seen on the road. (Stephen Dowle)

At the risk of showing similar vehicles in quick succession, this photograph of TWG 588 (MPD234), a similar Tiger Cub to the previous image, has been included to show an obvious panel of some sort behind the front wheel arch. I included an image in the *Dunfermline and West Fife's Trams and Buses* book of an AEC Reliance with a similar shaped glass panel, but even then, I was unsure of the purpose. Are these panels for emergency purposes perhaps? (Author's Collection)

Alexander C38F-bodied Leyland Tiger Cub RMS 711 (MPD222) was one of the first vehicles purchased by the new Alexander (Midland) company in July 1961, following the split up of the Alexander empire. It is seen parked up at Paton's Mill, Alloa, in June 1977, by which time it was Midland's oldest PSV licensed vehicle. It only lasted another four months before being withdrawn and sold on to a dealer in Glasgow. (Robert Dickson)

One of the coaches with the 1954 style of Alexander bodywork is seen here, parked up adjacent to Dundas Street bus station around the mid-1960s. Stepps-allocated Tiger Cub FMS 735 (MPD18) is on tour duty, an obvious assumption when the antimacassars are in place on the seat head rests. The prominent Bluebird logo can be seen on the rear wall of the bus station across the road. (Len Wright)

Our last look at the Leyland Tiger Cub shows us TWG 597 (MPD243). This is the same bus that was seen in an earlier photograph, coming off the ferry at Kyle of Lochalsh. This image, though, shows the bus with its original mirrors and no illuminated 'Pay as You Enter' display. It also makes an interesting comparison between door styles with RMS 704, the vehicle to its left, showing the later single-leaf coach door. (Len Wright)

Alexander (Midland) Leyland Leopard UMS 116J (MPE106) thunders up the hill out of Falkirk on its way on a local service 85 to Standburn. The summer of 1979 was a particularly pleasant one and on this day you could clearly see the Forth valley stretching down to the river itself, and beyond that to the Ochil Hills. (Dr George Fairbairn)

Seen belting along Princes Street in Edinburgh is Alexander (Midland) Leyland Leopard OSG 545M (MPE225). New to Scottish Omnibuses in 1974 and transferred to Alexander (Midland) in 1975, it is now revisiting its original home on a trip from Stirling. It is already screened for the return leg and will shortly be terminating at St Andrews Square bus station. (Dr George Fairbairn)

By the time this photograph was taken in August 1981, DMS 368C (MPE82) had become Alloa depot's oldest serving bus. It was new in 1965, making it sixteen years old, but it was not the only thing that was old as Alloa's bus station was beginning to look much run down by this date. It would only survive another three month before being closed down, with local services using the town centre. (Robert Dickson)

SSU 397R (MPE437) was a Leyland Leopard with a Duple Dominant E Type body, supplied new to Paton Brothers of Renfrew in November 1976. It passed to Western Scottish as YL8 in August 1979 and was allocated to Islay to run services abandoned by Maroner Coaches. When the SBG re-organised in 1985, the services and buses were transferred to Midland Scottish and this bus was re-numbered as MPE437. It is pictured here in Falkirk bus station in May 1986, carrying the fleet name 'Islay Midland Scottish'. See the next image for the continuing story of this bus. (Robert Dickson)

Unfortunately, all was not well with the bodywork on MPE437 and it was decided to re-body it using a scrapped ex-Fife Leopard in 1987. The bodywork from FPE62 (XXA 862M) was transferred onto the chassis of SSU 397R. This produced a useful vehicle, which continued in service. It is seen here with its new body in Falkirk bus station during July 1988, but three years later in 1991 it was acquired by Whitelaw's of Stonehouse. (Robert Dickson)

A good selection of vehicles was always guaranteed at Paton's Mill in Alloa, one of the area's main employers at the time. This was June 1980, and Alexander-bodied Leyland Leopard UMS 110J (MPE100) with dual purpose seating sits waiting patiently for its customers at the end of their shift. The blue was added to the skirt in 1978. (Robert Dickson)

Leyland Leopard TMS 411X (MPE411) takes a break in between runs on some local services in Falkirk during April 1985. It is seen wearing an in-house wrap-around advert displaying the price for a return journey between Falkirk and London. There is a picture of a similar advert applied to a Fife Leopard in the author's *Dunfermline & West Fife's Trams and Buses* book. (Robert Dickson)

School runs are traditionally done using double decker type vehicles as they are usually quite heavily loaded. Leyland Leopard GLS 289N (MPE219) is found to be more than capable in this instance when seen in May 1988, leaving Lornshill Academy in Alloa. I admit, it was good in those days to be able to drive with the door open on hot days to aid in the circulation of air, but it would certainly be frowned upon now. (Robert Dickson)

Midland Leopard GMS 306S (PE306) passes one of its Fife counterparts, CSF 167W (267), at Stirling bus station in preparation for the trip along the road to Alloa. The Midland vehicle still has a two-leaf door while the Fife vehicle has a four-leaf door and is fitted with dual purpose seats. (Clive A. Brown)

ULS 338T (MPE338) is pictured in Sauchie during May 1981on a service 62A from Alloa to Stirling via Tillicoultry. This bus was relatively new at the time, being only two years old, and looks very smart wearing a wrap-around advert for the Clydesdale Bank. To accommodate this advert, the fleet name was re-positioned to an area above the front two window bays. The fleet name would be in a similar position on the other side of the vehicle too. (Robert Dickson)

I hope the driver of AMS 290B (MPE24), a 1964 Alexander-bodied Leopard, notices that one of his side panels has worked loose and is swinging open while turning a corner. It is April 1979 and MPE24, a local Larbert-based vehicle, is seen working its way through Falkirk town centre on a local service. (Robert Dickson)

The Auld Kirk and the Barony Chambers form an impressive backdrop to GLS 271N (MPE201) as it heads off down the Cowgate, Kirkintilloch when photographed in July 1985, on a service 30A to Allandale. One of Midland's Metrobuses can be seen on the opposite side of the road wearing the 'Best Bus in Town' vinyls that a lot of the SBG companies were adopting in preparation for impending privatisation. (Robert Dickson)

In SBG days, many runs were shared between different operators. This was certainly the case with Midland and Fife, being in close proximity to each other and both being former Alexander companies. The 26A was one such service. GMS 309S (MPE309) had the honour on this particular day during April 1981. Travelling via Dunfermline, this service also took in Condorrat and Larbert. (Robert Dickson)

Grangemouth-allocated Leopard GMS 287S (MPE287) is pictured in Falkirk on the last day of May 1986, with what looks like a long journey ahead of it. Luckily, this California is merely a locale to the south of Falkirk. One of the company's MCW Metrobuses appears to be hot on his heels. (Robert Dickson)

Bridge of Allan sets a picturesque backdrop as ULS 330T (MPE330) makes its way through the village on a service 16 to Dundee, although I am positive that the service to Dundee through Bridge of Allan was in fact a service 15. The livery doesn't look right, with the cream extending from the lower skirt to the top of the windows. It would have been better stopping at the bottom of the windows. Perhaps this is in readiness for a wraparound style of advert. This would explain why the fleet name is in an independent cream panel above the first two windows. (Robert Dickson)

DMS 367C (MPE81) was fifteen years old when photographed hard at work in Sauchie in July 1980. It was running on a local 138 service between Alloa and Alva via Fishcross which was a half hourly service. By the time this vehicle was next known by the author in 1985, it had been converted into a tow wagon and was working with Kelvin Central Buses. (Robert Dickson)

This is ULS 715X (MPE415), an Alexander T Type Leyland Leopard, being hurled with great power towards Edinburgh's West End in 1984. The handsome blue and cream livery of Alexander (Midland) has been cast aside in the name of marketing and image and supplanted by a rather pale, striped Cityliner livery. The building in the left distance is Edinburgh Haymarket railway station. (Dr George Fairbairn)

Alexander AT Type Leyland Leopard RMS 401W (MPE401) of Kirkintilloch depot has just arrived at the former bus station in Carnegie Drive, Dunfermline, working through from Glasgow on a service 14A. Photographed in May 1983, this vehicle would join the Kelvin Scottish fleet two years later when Kirkintilloch was one of the depots to come under the jurisdiction of the new Kelvin company. (Clive A. Brown)

Midland Scottish Leyland Leopard ULS 334T (MPE334) takes centre stage in a scene reminiscent of the glory days of the Scottish Bus Group. Buchanan bus station plays host to vehicles from not just the Midland company, but also from the Central and Eastern Scottish companies. All the companies represented here now form part of the giant First Group company. Bus stations were certainly far more colourful places when the companies had their own individual liveries. (Stephen Dowle)

EMS 364V (364) was a Leyland Leopard with Alexander T Type bodywork. It was allocated to Bannockburn depot and wears the Midland Bluebird livery, as applied to this type of vehicle. It is seen here in Shillinghill, Alloa, as it makes haste on a local service 63 to Stirling. (Robert Dickson)

In 1991, Midland acquired this Alexander-bodied Leyland Leopard from Lothian Regional Transport. MSF 122P (462) was a fairly old bus, having been purchased new by Lothian in 1975, and filled a stop-gap in Midland's requirements at the time. It is unclear if the vehicle ever made it into the azure blue and cream livery of Midland Bluebird. The notice above the front nearside light cluster actually said 'Pay on entry', a Lothian application, but should have been totally removed before entering service with Midland. (Robert Dickson)

DLS 349V (PE349) was twelve years old by the time it was photographed here in Stirling bus station in 1991. This Leopard was an Alloa-allocated vehicle, but not for much longer as the depot in Alloa was about to close around this time. PE349 is seen with the traditional Midland Bluebird fleet name on the side of the vehicle, but sports a larger Bluebird gold-coloured logo above the front grille. (Robert Dickson)

Larbert depot in Falkirk is the location as we find RMS 400W (MPE400), a Leyland Leopard with Alexander T Type bodywork, at rest in between turns in April 1991. It was ten years old by this date and is seen sporting an alternative and little-used 'Bluebird' fleet name. It has been applied in blue on the cream front panel, and in gold on a blue coloured side panel. (Robert Dickson)

This was the style of application of the Midland Bluebird livery by the time the company was taken over by GRT Group in 1990. WFS 146W (454) is seen in its home depot of Larbert when photographed in September 1997. No. 454 was new to Fife Scottish Omnibuses in 1980 as their PE146, but was transferred to Midland Scottish Omnibuses in 1989. (Malcolm Audsley)

In 1970, Alexander (Midland) purchased seven Bedford VAS5 vehicles with Duple C29F bodywork. SMS 831H (MW291) was one of the batch and is seen about to leave Buchanan bus station on a peak time service in June 1979. Even with the lack of proper destination equipment, we know that it is on a service 177 as the typical SBG window sticker bears the name 'Woodhill', which was one of the termini in Auchinairn. Stationed at Kirkintilloch, this bus was apparently used for the early and late staff runs and was known as the staff bus. (Stephen Dowle)

One of the same type of coaches as seen in the previous photograph, SMS 829H (MW289) was allocated to Stepps depot and shows a variation in the application of the livery. The variation occurs between the roofline and the waistbands of both vehicles. I am unsure if each depot had their own interpretation of what the livery should be on these Bedford vehicles used for tour work. (Robert Dickson)

HWG 530E (MW274) was a Bedford VAM5 with Duple C45F body work, on hire to Scottish Omnibuses to help out at the 1976 Royal Highland Show at Ingliston. The Midland company had fifteen of these vehicles with Duple Viceroy body work, with all vehicles usually found on various extended tour and private hire work. (Dr George Fairbairn)

Another Duple-bodied Bedford with Alexander (Midland) was OYS 112F (MW304). It was acquired from David MacBrayne, Glasgow, in October 1970 with licences for coach tours from that city. It is seen here in the depot yard at St Andrews, Fife, sometime during the summer of 1976 while on tour duty. (Dr George Fairbairn)

Also purchased from David MacBrayne in 1970, is yet another Duple bodied Bedford, TGE 201G (MW306). The difference between these two vehicles is in the livery. Milngavie-based vehicle MW306 is seen to be wearing the reverse livery of MW304 from the roofline downwards. Both have the same style of seats, complete with obligatory antimacassars on the head rest areas. (Robert Dickson)

In 1974, Alexander (Midland) acquired two vehicles from Aberfeldy Motor Coaches. This one is TGS 221K (MW309), a Bedford YRQ with bodywork by Willowbrook to C45F layout. This vehicle was allocated to Crieff depot but is seen here in Alloa in June 1979 while working on a private hire. (Robert Dickson)

The second of the two former Aberfeldy Motor Coaches vehicles, WES 355L (MW310), was also a Bedford YRQ and also had body work by Willowbrook. Although both vehicles were new in 1972, but nine months apart, the body style has change quite a bit, with this vehicle fitted out to a B49F layout. The Willowbrook badge was quite a prominent feature on both these vehicles. (Robert Dickson)

Alloa town centre on Monday 2 November 1981. This was the day the buses started using the town centre instead of the ring road after the town's bus station had closed the day before. This photograph shows WMS 922J (MLH22), a Bristol LH with Alexander Y Type bodywork, travelling down the town's Drysdale Street on a local service 139 to Alva. (Robert Dickson)

The layover area at Stirling bus station sets the scene as we find Bristol LH WMS 921J (MLH21), which was ten years old when pictured in January 1981, resting in between turns on the service 54A. This was a local Stirling service, which ran between Cambusbarron and Woodside Road via King Street. (Robert Dickson)

Pictured in Stirling on a rather wet day in April 1984 is Alexander-bodied Daimler Fleetline SMS 127P (MRF127). New in July 1976, the Midland company always kept the black lining bordering the cream relief bands on their Alexander-bodied Fleetlines. I can't recall ever seeing the same treatment on any of the ECW or NC-bodied Fleetlines in the Midland fleet. (Robert Dickson)

Midland's sister company, Alexander (Fife), operated five Daimler Fleetlines with bodywork by Northern Counties. They were new to Fife in 1971 but weren't liked there and all five were moved to Midland in 1975. Here, SXA 71K (MRF106) is pictured in Falkirk bus station eleven years later, having dropped its passengers off while on a local service. (Robert Dickson)

Here is one of the later Eastern Coach Works-bodied Fleetlines, although by the date of the photograph, October 1980, it has now been re-badged as a Leyland. This vehicle is ULS 670T (MRF145), and is seen in Falkirk town centre on a traditionally wet autumn day on a local service 99 between Westquarter and Langlees. (Robert Dickson)

This photograph is included as a study of Fleetline rear end styles. From left to right, we have: ULS 675T (MRF150), an Eastern Coach Works-bodied Leyland Fleetline; next, wearing a wide cream relief band, we have the first of three Alexander bodied vehicles, which is LMS 165W (MRF165), another Fleetline bearing a Leyland badge; the last two vehicles are both Daimlers in the shape of NWG 5G (MRF62) and KWG 366F (MRF36). This photograph was taken in Grangemouth depot in September 1980. (Robert Dickson)

Another photograph that clearly shows the black lining applied to the cream relief bands on the Fleetline. HWG 507E (MRF8) was found resting in Stirling depot when photographed in April 1980, still wearing the twin relief bands as originally applied in 1967 when new. It appears that a small advert beside the destination display has been removed rather promptly, taking a large area of paintwork with it. (Robert Dickson)

I always thought that the Alexander style of body work looked very smart and incorporated the rear end dome of the Y Type body quite ingeniously. The only thing the marred the Midland Fleetlines was the extremely large fog lamp on the lower nearside front panel. It is clearly seen in this image of SMS 406H (MRF76), waiting on the workers from Paton's Mill in Alloa in July 1982. (Robert Dickson)

Around 1981–2, many Alexander-bodied Fleetlines and Ailsa buses in the Fife and Midland operating areas were appearing with large cream bands between the lower and upper saloons. I believe this was an attempt to freshen up the liveries in readiness for privatisation. LMS 155W (MRF155), a 1980 Fleetline, is wearing this experimental livery when seen in Perth depot in April 1982. (Robert Dickson)

Nine Midland Scottish Daimler Fleetlines are seen here parked up in Marine Garage, Portobello, Edinburgh, on a private hire in 1981, most probably for that year's Royal Highland Show. Almost all are Alexander-bodied examples, but that nearest the

camera is an ex-Central SMT ECW-bodied bus, and third from the far end, we can just make out a Northern Counties-bodied vehicle. The Midland shade of blue, when viewed en masse, seems to enhance the appearance of the vehicles. (Dr George Fairbairn)

Another visit to the popular Hillfoots town of Alva. Buses could usually be seen here from places such as Fife, Glasgow and Edinburgh, as well as the local buses from Midland. They would usually be transporting Sunday school kids or other private hire groups to the town for picnicking. Nearest the camera, HWG 510E (MRF11) compares well with SMS 127P (MRF127), with the different roof profiles and the destination and windscreen areas being at different levels too. (Robert Dickson)

The upper saloon area of Eastern Coach Works-bodied Daimler Fleetline TGM 225J (MRF118), is seen clearly from this high viewing point. The bus was new to Central SMT as their D25 in July 1971, but was acquired just over four years later by Alexander (Midland). It is seen in Alloa in October 1983, working a local 64A service to Sauchie. (Robert Dickson)

When you look at this photograph, you see three Alexander-bodied Daimler Fleetlines parked up in Balfron depot in June 1984. They are, from the left, SMS 123P (MRF123), SMS 125P (MRF125) and SMS 401H (MRF71). Upon closer inspection, you begin to notice the slight variations between the various registration plates, fleet number styles, fog lamps and roof dome styles. This might be of no importance to most people, but are the things that modellers like to be aware of. (Robert Dickson)

Another photograph that gives us a look at another couple of minor variations. These two Larbert-based, Alexander-bodied Fleetlines are LMS 751W (751) and LMS 766W (766) and they are seen in Falkirk bus station in March 1992. New in 1980 as MRF 151/166 and in the normal Midland Scottish livery at the time, the livery has now been altered to extend the cream relief band down to the bottom of the lower saloon windows. The cream even extends around the whole of the doorway of 751 on the left. The former 'Pay as You Enter' sign on the front panel of 751 has also received paintwork. (Robert Dickson)

Larbert-based Daimler Fleetline SMS 403H (MRF73) passes through Falkirk on a local 95 service to Hallglen, a local estate to the south of the town. This vehicle was new in 1970, and was, of course, built on the opposite side of the town at the Walter Alexander factory in Camelon. Photographed in 1986, the bus livery seen here has the cream relief band extended down to the bottom of the lower saloon windows. (Robert Dickson)

This front nearside view gives us a good look at the entry/exit door area and reminds us that the stairs to the upper saloon on these buses faced rearward. This ECW-bodied Fleetline is TGM 224J (MRF115) and was another of the buses that came from Central SMT in 1975. Based in Kirkintilloch, it has brought a load of families through to Alva on a Sunday school outing in May 1981. (Robert Dickson)

This 1980 image of ULS 663T (MRF138), seen in Glasgow on a local service to Drumchapel, shows the rich blue colour of the Midland livery off nicely. By this time, Fleetlines were no longer Daimlers and the company was now Midland Scottish, but change isn't all that bad when one looks at the grimy, run-down state of the buildings in the background. (Dr George Fairbairn)

Our last group photograph of Fleetlines shows two of the ECW-bodied vehicles parked up at their home depot in Bannockburn during September 1990. Having been renumbered the previous year, ULS 664T (RF739) and ULS 662T (RF737) sit side-by-side to let us see the different fleet number styles and the replaced upper saloon front windows on RF739. (Robert Dickson)

Leyland Fleetline ULS 672T (747) with ECW bodywork is seen parked up at Falkirk bus station in August 1992, not too long before its withdrawal from service. It was new in 1979 as MRF147 and was allocated to Larbert depot. This bus appears to have had its original upper front opening windows replaced by more traditional plain glass, similar to RF739 in the previous photograph. (Robert Dickson)

We start our look at the Ford vehicles with, appropriately, PWG 467M (MT1). This bus was new in April 1974 and had Duple Dominant body work to a C41F layout. It is seen here outside its home depot in Stirling in July 1981 while out of service, although it was initially based at Kirkintilloch. The destination display on this vehicle was located below the windscreen. (Robert Dickson)

Next, we move up to the 'Fair City' of Perth as we see one of their Fords hard at work on a very wet day during July 1981. This vehicle, MMS 332P (MT32), was new in September 1975 and was bodied by Alexander to a B45F layout. One of the company's Daimler Fleetlines is seen hot on the heels of MT32 as it makes its way on a local service 34 to Muirton, to the north of the city centre. (Robert Dickson)

On a visit to Alloa in February 1983, RLS 51P (MT51) was found lurking away at the rear of the depot. What it was doing there is uncertain as the vehicle appears to be allocated to Cumbernauld depot and was only seven years old at the time. As it was parked up beside some withdrawn Fife Fleetlines, it may have been getting prepared to be moved on to another operator. It seated forty-five passengers inside the Duple Dominant body and had the destination display in the more familiar position above the windscreen. (Robert Dickson)

Another Duple Dominant-bodied Ford, but with forty-nine seats, is pictured on a more mundane task as it works away on a run from Alloa to Stirling on a service 62A. The location is Sauchie, north of Alloa, one of the intermediate stopping locations for this service. With a modicum of passengers on board, a young mother makes light work of disembarking with a pushchair and baby. Not many low floored buses in those days, but no one bothered about it. (Robert Dickson)

Larbert-allocated RLS 466T (MT66), another of the Alexander-bodied Fords, with a B45F layout, is seen resting in between runs at Falkirk bus station in August 1985. This 1979-built vehicle shows a different arrangement to the front grille area and included Ford lettering. It was allocated to Crieff depot when it passed to the new Strathtay Scottish group and was last known to be rotting away at an undisclosed location on the Isle of Lewis. (Robert Dickson)

RMS 602M (MT2) was a Duple-bodied Ford with coach seating for forty-one passengers. This image clearly shows that these vehicles had four skylights, as they are all shown in the open position when MT2 was photographed parked up in Stirling bus station, shortly after its addition to the fleet in 1974. (Paul Redmond)

This Alexander Y Type Ford, NLS 943P (MT43), had a larger chassis and was built with Alexander's standard B53F bodywork. Allocated to Alloa depot, it is pictured exiting from the town's bus station in July 1980, on a short hop to the west towards Tullibody via Inglewood. Inglewood is a leafy, local suburb just to the west of Alloa bus station. I am unsure what lurked behind the small flap seen in the company logo between the word 'Midland' and the three-quarter Saltire. (Robert Dickson)

Our first look at the Seddon Pennine 7 shows us KSX 671N (MSE3) sitting on stance at Bo'ness bus station in October 1987. This bus was new in 1975 to Eastern Scottish Omnibuses and ran as their ZS671 until it was transferred to Midland Scottish in June 1985. It ran from Linlithgow depot, which up until the mid-1980s had been under Eastern Scottish control. Linlithgow depot was transferred to Midland Scottish in preparation for the deregulation, and eventual privatisation, of the Scottish bus industry. (Robert Dickson)

Another vehicle from the same batch seen in the previous image makes its way through Linlithgow on a local service with another stable mate in hot pursuit. KSX 680N (MSE6) ran as ZS680 in the fleet of Eastern Scottish, the letter Z denoting the fact that the vehicle used 'dual purpose' seating. Midland Scottish liked to enclose a lot of their fleet names in a rectangular housing, as can be seen here on the front of the bus. (Robert Dickson)

Alexander AYS-bodied Seddon Pennine 7 JFS 983X (MSE27) sits at rest in the layover area at Stirling bus station in between runs on a service 38 to Linlithgow. JFS 983X was new to Scottish Omnibuses in 1982 as their S983, but was transferred to Midland Scottish in June 1985, only three months before being photographed here. It would soon be re-painted into the standard Midland Scottish livery at the time. (Robert Dickson)

LSC 941T (SE521) was another of those Y Type Seddon Pennines from Scottish Omnibuses. This one was a bit older though, being new in 1971 as their S941. This vehicle was also acquired by Midland Scottish in 1985 and was re-numbered MSE21. In 1989, it was renumbered once again to SE521, the guise it wears when seen here in its home depot of Bannockburn in February 1991. Note the positioning of the corporate fleet name on the plated-over grille area. (Robert Dickson)

Midland Scottish never ordered any new Seddon Pennine buses themselves, relying on vehicles acquired from other operators. The bulk of these buses came from Eastern Scottish Omnibuses, but a few made their way from Western, Kelvin and Clydeside. Most were bodied by Alexander with the short window Y Type body but GSX 873T (MSE8), pictured here, was given the T Type body. New in 1978 as Eastern's ZS873, it was transferred to Midland in June 1985 and remained allocated to Linlithgow depot as it was the depot that technically transferred. It is pictured in its home town in October 1987 on a service 38 to Edinburgh. (Robert Dickson)

New to Midland Scottish in 1983, Alexander-bodied Leyland Tiger BMS 515Y (MPT115) is seen in Fort William bus station in August 1984 in between runs to and from Glasgow on a feeder service for the London Express buses. A collection of parcels is either waiting to be placed in the bus or has just been removed from the bus. Services like these tended to reach Glasgow to connect to the London-bound services from Buchanan bus station. (Robert Dickson)

Duple Laser-bodied Leyland Tiger A130 ESG (MPT130) was new in June 1984 and was branded in the livery of Scottish Citylink. It only wore the Citylink livery for a short time before being re-liveried with brandings for 'National Holidays'. It was seen here approaching Buchanan bus station in October 1985 with an almost full complement of passengers. (Robert Dickson)

ALS 101Y (MPT101) was a Leyland Tiger with Alexander AT Type body. This was a good combination of chassis and body for longer distance inter-urban duties. MPT101 is seen here at rest in the layover area at Falkirk bus station in February 1983 when only about one month old. The Leyland badges are quite prominently shown on the front panel area. (Robert Dickson)

Alloa depot is the location as we find BLS 108Y (MPT108) lurking on the side road to the rear of the yard. This bus was new to Midland Scottish in 1983 as MPT108, but was transferred to Kelvin Scottish, on short loan, as their T108C in June 1985. It was returned to Midland in March 1986, just a few days before it was photographed here. This Leyland Tiger is sporting Duple Dominant 2 C47F body work, but the livery style doesn't look very flattering. (Robert Dickson)

The Leyland Tiger was a chassis well suited for long distance work and, when combined with an Alexander TE type of body, was well suited for tour and private hire work. New in 1983 with the registration BMS 514Y, MPT114 has now been re-registered as FSU334 and is seen parked up in Kincardine in June 1990. It is wearing the 'Bluebird Express' branding with the (in my view), not very convincing Bluebird emblem at this time. (Robert Dickson)

SSU 827 (PT147) is a Leyland Tiger which started its life in 1982 with Eastern Scottish Omnibuses as their XCL 554 and a Duple Goldliner III body. Between Eastern and Midland ownership in 1988, it spent a short time with Kelvin as their 4326 and somewhere along the line had its body work upgraded to a Goldliner IV model. It is in this guise that it is pictured here in Stirling bus station in September 1992, wearing Scottish Citylink colours. (Robert Dickson)

This was one of the original Mk 1 Leyland Nationals that were bought by Midland Scottish in 1978. OLS 806T (MPN6) is pictured outside Stirling depot in October 1980, wearing an advert for the old Graham & Morton store, which that year was celebrating 150 years of service. To accommodate the advert, the company fleet name was moved to the roofline area above the entrance door. (Robert Dickson)

Looking from Alloa bus station on 1 May 1984, with the Town Hall in the background, we find bus JPA 125K, having just arrived from Tillicoultry. This was one of Mackie's buses, acquired to operate the former Halley service from Alloa to Tillicoultry. Mackie's had taken over Halley's business and had painted this bus in the traditional Halley livery. Today, the bus station area is now the location of the local police station. One of Midland's Mk 2 Leyland Nationals, NLS 982W (MPN30), is also seen in the bus station and has its 'Pay on Entry' sign illuminated. (Robert Dickson)

The date is now November 1984 and the same vehicle, NLS 982W (MPN30), is seen within Stirling bus station. During the six months between dates, MPN30 has now gained an alteration to help improve the airflow into the engine compartment. It is seen on the rear near side corner and looks similar to a periscope type of design. (Robert Dickson)

Another bus from the first batch of Leyland National Mk 1s sitting within the confines of its home depot is OLS 812T (MPN12). This one also seems to be sporting an additional improvement to the air cooling within the engine compartment. One of Fife's Mk 2 Nationals also had this improvement added to it and is shown on page 71 of the author's *Fife Buses* book. (Robert Dickson)

Midland's first Leyland Nationals arrived in 1978, when fifteen of the Mk 1 type arrived. The first five of this batch had roof mounted heater pods and 'Pay as You Enter' illuminated signs. The following ten were just to the standard Mk 1 design. OLS 801T (MPN1) was the first of the batch and is seen here in September 1980 outside Paton's Mill, Alloa, ready for the workforce to come out at the end of the dayshift. (Robert Dickson)

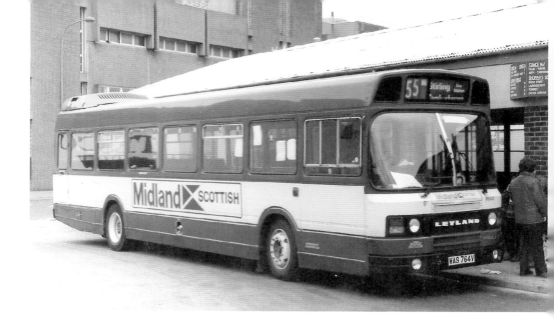

WAS 764V (PN44) displays the type of Midland Scottish logo that was being applied to the second-hand Leyland National Mk 2s at the end of the 1980s. The size was similar to the logos being used by Fife Scottish buses at the time too. The bus has just arrived in Stirling bus station on a local service 55 at the end of March 1990. New to Highland in 1980, it was acquired by Kelvin Scottish in 1986. It was acquired by Midland the following year and re-seated to forty-nine in October 1989. (Robert Dickson)

It is quite easy to see how the Midland Scottish livery evolved from the traditional blue and cream to its application when the company was calling itself Midland Bluebird. With the mere addition of the upward sweep from the rear wheel arch to the roof, you have the basis for the livery in the next photograph. Mk 1 National OLS 815T (MPN15), new in 1978, is pictured in Alloa bus station in March 1987, wearing Midland's adapted version of the SBG slogan 'Best Bus with us'. (Robert Dickson)

Mk 1 Leyland National OLS 814T (14) is a sister vehicle to the bus in the previous photograph, coming from the same batch in 1978. It is pictured in Falkirk bus station in March 1992, wearing the final version of the inherent Midland livery. For a Leyland National of any type to last in a fleet for fourteen years was quite a feat considering the problems they had with rusting. (Robert Dickson)

Midland's Perth depot was the first to receive the highbridge Volvo Ailsa in May 1977. Fourteen were delivered as part of a diverted Fife order and all were allocated to Perth. YMS 702R (MRA2) is seen hard at work on a wet day in July 1981, working its way through the busy city centre on a local service to North Muirton. (Robert Dickson)

Six months after the date of the previous image and the Ailsas have now been moved to other Midland depots in the central belt. On 2 November 1981, YMS 712R (MRA12), now allocated to Alloa depot, is seen in Drysdale Street on a service 62 to Stirling via Tillicoultry. Alloa bus station had closed the previous day as Alloa town centre was going through a bit of a redevelopment at that time. (Robert Dickson)

These school kids look a bit over excited as they are taken home at the end of the school day on Ailsa YMS 705R (MRA5). This is another Alloa depot Ailsa and the school is Lornshill Academy, to the west of the town. The date is March 1983 and this particular vehicle is already starting to look a bit worse for wear and in need of a repaint to freshen it up. (Robert Dickson)

At first glance, this looks like a Midland Scottish vehicle. But the truth is given away by the red background on both the fleet number and shed code plates. This is Fife Scottish Ailsa OSC 65V (FRA65), which was on loan to Midland to take part in comparative trials, hence the prominent TB3 on the roundel between decks. It is pictured in a desolate cityscape opposite Buchanan bus station, Glasgow, in 1980. (Dr George Fairbairn)

D602 FLS (MMS602) was an Orion-bodied Sherpa minibus allocated to Midland's Oban depot. Midland Scottish only had two of these vehicles, which were new in October 1986. They were both transferred to the new Oban & District company on its formation in 1992. MMS602 is seen here outside the Bank of Scotland building in Station Road, Oban. (Malcolm Jones)

H925 PMS (625) was a Reeve-Burgess-bodied Mercedes-Benz minibus, which was new to Midland Scottish in November 1990. It is seen here in a rather wet Stirling town centre on a local service 155 to Cornton, probably the type of service that suited these twenty-five seater minibuses. (Author's Collection)

Another of the minibus combinations used by Midland was this Mercedes-Benz with Alexander's twenty-one seat, earlier AM style of body work. It was new to Kelvin Scottish as their 1102 in 1986, but was moved on the following year to Midland. C102 KDS (MMB622), allocated to Alloa depot, is seen here in the town's bus station in April 1987, working a local service to Rosebank, Sauchie. (Robert Dickson)

In March 1987, Midland Scottish bought new MCW minibuses to work on the new town services around Alloa. On the first day of these new services, a trio of the new buses was seen parked up at the town's bus station. The buses are, from left, D650 GLS (MM654), D648 GLS (MM652) and D647 GLS (MM651). As can be seen, the Bluebird logo was quite prominent on the sides of these vehicles, with the corporate fleet name emblazoned along the front below the windscreen. (Robert Dickson)

J776 WLS (639) was another combination of Mercedes-Benz chassis with Alexander's bodywork. The styling has been slightly altered on this later AM style and it is fitted with twenty-three dual purpose seats. It was new in December 1991 to Midland Scottish and is seen here two years later in Falkirk, on a local service 98 to Tamfourhill, a residential suburb about a mile and a half to the west of the town centre. (Author's Collection)

At the Greater Glasgow PTE open day in April 1978, Metro-Cammell Weymann showed off this Metrobus in the livery of Alexander (Midland). The Midland company must have been impressed with this vehicle as they took it in great numbers shortly afterwards, although not necessarily with this body work, as a replacement for the Daimler Fleetline. This particular vehicle was later sold to China Motor Bus. (Dr George Fairbairn)

UMS 751T (MRM1) was the first of the Metrobuses bought by Midland Scottish in April 1979, one year after the demonstrator was seen in Glasgow. This one had Alexander AD Type bodywork with an H43/30F layout and was stationed at Milngavie depot. Notice the original 'Metrobus' plate on the front grille which would be replaced by the more traditional 'MCW' plate. (Paul Redmond)

It would be a further four months before the second Metrobus, BLS 671V (MRM2), would make its appearance (August 1979). Once again, the Alexander AD style of bodywork was used with the H43/30F layout. This bus was also allocated to Milngavie depot and was more often than not found on the service 105 between Glasgow City Centre and Drumchapel with its 'older' sister, MRM1. (Clive A. Brown)

By the time B94 PKS (MRM94) was pictured in Falkirk bus station in May 1986, the Alexander bus body had changed to the RL Type and the livery application was somewhat different too. The cream band between upper and lower saloons had been lowered to incorporate the lower saloon windows. The bus also carries one of the SBG slogans of the time, 'Best Bus in Town'. (Robert Dickson)

Another six years have passed and although the livery is the same, B102 PKS (MRM102) is seen, again in Falkirk bus station, sporting the gold-coloured Bluebird fleet name that was seen earlier in the book. This bus was new in 1985 but spent a short time with Kelvin before returning once more to Midland. (Robert Dickson)

Another step in the evolution of the Metrobus and its livery style. E618 NLS (MRM118) was new to Midland Scottish in 1987, with a new front panel style to the RL type of body. When pictured here in Stirling bus station in March 1989, the livery had been changed to incorporate a large 'Bluebird' logo and some upward sweeping inclines near the rear wheel arch. (Robert Dickson)

ULS 643X (843) was nineteen years old when it was seen leaving Stirling bus station in 2001 on a service 60 to Clackmannan. It is evident how the basic Midland livery evolved along with the various eras and takeovers. The livery application seen on this bus while with First is plainly inherited from the livery seen in the previous photograph of MRM118. (Robert Dickson)

Our final look at the Metrobus shows us B581 MLS (881) in the final livery to be seen on a Midland Metrobus. No. 881 was new in September 1984 to Midland Scottish and was over twenty years old when seen on a local service around Stirling. The Metrobus proved in the end that it was a good replacement vehicle for the Fleetline and lasted a lot longer. (Bob Dickson)

We often see many bus photographs that have been taken in various bus depots, but not too many photographs of the depots themselves. This photograph gives us a general view of the yard area at Bannockburn depot. This was taken in April 1995 and gives us an idea of the type of vehicles housed in that depot at the time. The Leyland Leopard and the Metrobus seem to be the principal vehicle types found at Bannockburn. (Robert Dickson)

Balfron depot is shown here during a visit in June 1984. You tend to get the impression of a busy and compact small depot which is situated off Dunmore Street. As with the previous photograph, two vehicle types stand out in this depot also. Again, the Leyland Leopard stands out as being the only single deck type on view, with the Daimler Fleetline being the prevalent double decked type. (Robert Dickson)

Midland Scottish buses were frequently found on services outwith the traditional areas associated with the company. This is a typical scene in Dundee bus station in the 1980s as buses from all three former Alexander companies make use of the facilities. Notice the difference between the waistbands of the Northern and Fife vehicles, with Northern retaining the stepped waistband and the Fife Leopard wearing a straight waistband. The Midland vehicle is Leyland Leopard EMS 363V (MPE363), with the Alexander AT type of body work. (Clive A. Brown)

New to Midland Bluebird in May 1994, Wright-bodied Scania N113 L553 HMS (553) is captured within the confines of Larbert depot three years later. I never liked this livery very much as it made the traditional livery, used by Alexander's, seem so long ago in the past. This vehicle was noted in Dunsmore's scrap yard, Larkhall, in  February 2008, having not long been withdrawn from service. (Malcolm Audsley)

L552 GMS (52) was a Mercedes-Benz O405 which had Wright Cityranger body work. It was new to Midland Bluebird in August 1993 and is seen here not long after purchase, in stance 7 at Stirling bus station on an inter-urban service 63 to Fallin. The livery would have been further enhanced had there been more blue applied either around the roofline or the skirt area. (Author's Collection)

ORS 208R (708) represents one of twenty five Alexander AL-bodied Leyland Atlanteans that were moved from the main Grampian fleet in the early 1990s. No. 708 was new in 1977 as Grampian's 208 but was photographed here in August 1992, five months after arrival, in Falkirk bus station. The central doors on these vehicles were never used by Midland Bluebird. (Robert Dickson)

Plaxton Paramount-bodied Leyland Tiger F622 WXY (190) was new to Yorkshire Rider in 1988 and subsequently passed on to Bradford Traveller. It is seen in Larbert Depot in September 1997 while on loan to Midland Bluebird. It is unknown how long this vehicle was operated on loan or what the reason was for the bus shortage at Midland Bluebird. (Malcolm Audsley)

New to First West Yorkshire in 1996, this Northern Counties-bodied Volvo, P535 EFL (34015), shows off to good effect the First Midland Bluebird livery as applied before the fade-out pink was done away with, and the swirl above the rear wheel arch incorporated into the livery. It was photographed negotiating the roundabout outside Stirling Railway Station in March 2007, working a service 60 from Clackmannan. (Robert Dickson)

R448 ALS (518) is a Wright Access Ultralow Scania L113 and was new to Yorkshire Rider in 1998. This is a Balfron-allocated vehicle, proudly displaying 'Midland Bluebird' below the driver's cab window. It is seen here in Falkirk town centre on an old local service 77, which is now registered as a Hawick town service. (Author's Collection)

A general look at some of the company's vehicles in the layover area at Falkirk bus station at the end of December 1992. From left to right we find 'Y' type Leopard, TMS 410X (410) parked next to Alexander bodied Fleetline LMS 155W (755). Another two Alexander bodied Leopards, both with 'T' type bodies in the shape of EMS 362V (362) and HSU 301 (268). Somewhere along the line, HSU 301 was re-registered from GLS 268S and gained a more modern 'TE' type of lower front panel. Last, but not least is former Highland and Kelvin Mk2 Leyland National, WAS 764V (44). All these vehicles were allocated to Larbert depot. (Robert Dickson)

Two contrasting styles of livery application are seen on these two Mercedes Benz buses with early Wright bodywork. New in August 1993 to Midland Bluebird, L555 GMS (62315) and L556 GMS (62316) are seen side-by-side, sitting within the confines of Balfron depot, in the spring of 2006. (Robert Dickson)

Typical of the vehicles used by First at present, we find R448 ALS (62305), a 1998 Wright-bodied Scania N113. This vehicle was purchased from Yorkshire Rider when only about two months old and is seen here, working from Balfron depot, on a local service through Bridge of Allan on a circular run also taking in Stirling and Cowie. (Robert Dickson)

Photographed near Stirling bus station in April 2007, we find SN54 KFE (65722), a Wright Eclipse Solar-bodied Scania wearing branding for the city's 'Unilink' service between the university and the city centre. This bus was new in February 2005 and wore this livery for some years. It is now to be seen in the more traditional FirstBus colours. (Robert Dickson)

One of First Midland Bluebird's Volvo B7s with Wright bodywork, SN09 FBB (69406), is seen passing Larbert depot during September 2013 on one of the limited run services operated by the company at present. New in 2009, this vehicle wears an attractive, dedicated branding livery for the X38 service, which runs between Stirling and Edinburgh. (David McGeachan)

KWG 623 was new in 1958 as RD70 and worked at Perth depot. This LD6G Lodekka ran in the red livery of the Perth City fleet. It was withdrawn in 1975 and used as service vehicle ML276, for use as a mobile scaffolding unit and as an un-licensed trailer. It was being used internally at Grangemouth depot when photographed here in June 1976. (Robert Dickson)

A bit of history goes with this training vehicle. It is a Metro-Cammell bodied Leyland Titan PD3A/1 and was new in 1961 to Leicester Corporation as their 246 and bore the registration number 246AJF. It was acquired by Eastern Scottish as a driver trainer around 1985/6 and was re-registered as BHN740B at the same time. Midland Scottish acquired it in 1987, also for driver training, and gave it the fleet number ML326. It is pictured here in Falkirk in October 1989, but was withdrawn by the end of 1991. It was sold to PSV Sales, Barnsley, and was purchased in 1992 for use as a traveller's home and moved from site to site before ending up in Normandy, France. The owner died and it was left to rot in a yard in Brittany, still wearing these colours applied by Midland Scottish. (Robert Dickson)

ONG 353F was a driver training vehicle that had been bought by Midland Scottish just for that purpose. It was new in 1968 to Eastern National as their FLF 353 but was acquired by Eastern Scottish in 1973 as part of a Bristol VRT/FLF swap similar to that which Midland had done a couple of years previously. Midland acquired the bus in 1982 and converted it straight into a driver training vehicle and it is seen here two years later in 1984. (Robert Dickson)

The trainer must have been having a tea break with his trainees when Leyland Leopard XMS 244R was spotted in the layover area at Falkirk bus station in August 1992. New in March 1977 as part of a diverted order for Western SMT, it received the fleet number MPE244 and was again renumbered as PE244 in 1989 and just plain old 244 in 1990. Having just been used for driver training duties, it was renumbered again to 921, as seen here. The vehicle is still in service bus livery, but is seen to be suitably adorned with 'L' plates. (Robert Dickson)

0202 MS (179), seen here in Larbert depot, was a Leyland TD4, new to Walter Alexander & Sons in 1935. It had been registered as WG 3383 with the fleet number R49 until withdrawal in April 1948, when it was converted to a service lorry. The Leyland L27/26R body was sold to a dealer in Falkirk and the lorry body from L142 (MS9031) was fitted. It was after this conversion that it ran on trade plate 0202 MS. It was sold to a Glasgow dealer in 1969. (Paul Redford)

May 1978 sees Midland breakdown vehicle GM 5875 (ML245) leaving Buchanan bus station, having attended to a failed Bristol FLF Lodekka. It was rebuilt from an all-Leyland Titan PD2/1 which had been new in 1953 to Central SMT as their L475. This vehicle survives to this day and can be found in preservation at Birkenhead. (Stephen Dowle)

One of Midland's tow wagons is pictured in Stirling bus station in October 1989, having just attended to a minor problem. DMS 330C is a Leyland Leopard, new in 1965 as MPE 45, and has Alexander Y Type bodywork. Believed to have been converted around 1980, it received the fleet number L903 and ran on trade plates. At some point in the 1980s, it was fitted with a later style front panel and re-numbered as ML 302. The livery looks not too dissimilar to that used by Fife Scottish in the mid-1980s and sports a red corporate fleet name. (Robert Dickson)

By way of comparison, here we see a sister vehicle of that shown in the previous photograph. Milngavie depot allocated ML 303 is seen with its original front panel and shows the cut away area in the front grille that was necessary to accommodate the towing eye. (Author's Collection)

Our first look at life after Midland for some of the fleet as we find HMS 10, an LD6G Lodekka which was new in 1956 to the Lawson's fleet as RD25. This bus was withdrawn in 1972 and was sold to Stirlingshire Road Safety Committee in September that year. It is seen here nine years later with a rather smart Central Scotland Police white colour scheme, still promoting road safety. (Robert Dickson)

NWG 13G was new to Alexander (Midland) in July 1968 as their MRF70. I have no record of when it was withdrawn, but it had obviously seen further use as a mobile workshop with Clackmannan District Council when seen in Alloa in July 1985. It was, on this occasion, joined by another ex-Midland Fleetline, MWG 780F (MRF48), which served the same purpose but was just out of shot. (Robert Dickson)

Midland Scottish made good use of Alexander-bodied Bristol LH SMS 675H after it was withdrawn from service work in 1981. New in May 1970 as MLH5 in the Midland fleet, it is seen 'working' in Alloa bus station as the company's 'Information Bus' but now carries the fleet number ML308. One cannot deny that this special livery was quite eye catching. (Robert Dickson)

SWG 679H was another Alexander-bodied LH and was new in June 1970 with the fleet number MLH19. This one was also withdrawn around 1981 and, as can be seen when it was photographed in Stirling in 1983, it was donated to Radio Royal Hospital Broadcasting, which broadcast to the hospitals in Stirling and Falkirk. The legend on the side of the roof panels states that the vehicle was 'Donated in Memory of Walter Alexander'. Don't you think the stripes make the vehicle very 'Stagecoach' looking? (Robert Dickson)

The rear area at Alloa depot was used to store buses that were awaiting disposal or transfer to other operators. Fife vehicles were often found here, but on this occasion at the end of 1980, we can see a general view of the yard area with about fourteen de-licensed Albion Vikings on view. The one nearest the camera was JMS 443E (MNV30). Alloa depot was situated next to the west side of Alloa Athletics' Recreation Park. (Robert Dickson)

Almost a year later from the previous photograph and we find ourselves still within Alloa depot. This time, we are looking towards the railway footbridge from which the last image was recorded. A great variety of withdrawn vehicles are on show, including one of the company's Lodekka training buses, a couple of Bristol LH chassis types, a Duple-bodied coach, and a myriad of other Alexander-bodied vehicles. (Robert Dickson)

This is all that remained of Albion Vikings EMS 93C (MNV4) and EMS 191C (MNV8) when they were photographed here at the rear of Alloa depot in November 1979. They had been practically stripped to the bone for spare parts to enable the other vehicles to stay on the road. At least they were put to some sort of good use. Even the driver's seat on the left chassis has gone, but the chassis on the right looks like it could be sitting in Walter Alexander's factory, just waiting for a new body. (Robert Dickson)

A lot of Midland vehicles ended their lives here in Larbert depot. This is all that remains of Leyland Titan PD3/3 OMS299 (MRB 225) when it was photographed in August 1976, only a few months after withdrawal. It was new to Walter Alexander in 1960 and transferred in 1961 to the new Midland company, where it spent its entire life. (Robert Dickson)